# In Hampshire's Skies

Front cover: Providing an intriguing example of the innovative work undertaken by the Royal Aircraft Factory at Farnborough in the First World War is this Vickers Gunbus armament installation. Two Vickers machine guns are shown mounted astride a moveable searchlight powered from the rather prominent wind-driven generator. Though appearing potent, this early forerunner of today's 'search and destroy' systems was not adopted for wide service use. (SHA)

# IN HAMPSHIRE'S SKIES

*Colin Cruddas*

TEMPUS

First published 2001
Copyright © Colin Cruddas, 2001

Tempus Publishing Limited
The Mill, Brimscombe Port,
Stroud, Gloucestershire, GL5 2QG

ISBN 0 7524 2140 9

Typesetting and origination by
Tempus Publishing Limited
Printed in Great Britain by
Midway Colour Print, Wiltshire

www.tempus-publishing.com
www.arcadiapublishing.com

Michael Turner's evocative painting of the Farnborough F1 shows the aircraft which Richard Noble's design team are confident will break the last commercial aviation frontier. Conceived specifically to shorten the time of business travel, the F1, entirely computer designed and using modern composite construction techniques will, it is predicted, recover volume aircraft production in Great Britain. For more details of this unique concept, access website www.farnborough-aircraft.com (FA)

# Contents

# Acknowledgements

I am deeply grateful to the following friends and colleagues who gave so freely of their time and expert knowledge in the preparation of this book.

My special thanks go to Fawley Historians Colin van Geffen, Dave Etheridge and Clare Murley, not only for providing so much invaluable personal assistance and material but also for giving me free access to the Peter New Photographic Collection. Barry Guess and Mike Fielding of BAE Systems Heritage have cheerfully and unfailingly met what I am sure have been totally unreasonable demands for photographic assistance, as indeed have Phil Moody and Mike Slade in opening up the Farnborough Air Sciences Trust (FAST) archive and Mark Gibb in providing so much material on Southampton's Airport. Peerless in their respective fields, are Alan Brown (New Forest Airfields) and Christopher Balfour (Portsmouth Airport and associated companies) and I hope that what appears here represents a fair digest of their collective and most welcome contributions. Mike Phipp has, as on so many previous occasions, proved to be the man who, if not knowing the answer to an awkward question himself, can invariably point me towards someone who does – and it doesn't get any better than that!

For filling in most of the gaps (due to restricted space many will still appear), my sincere appreciation goes to Colonel Derek Armitage (Museum of Army Flying), Mike Dempsey (Farnborough Aircraft), Richard Gardner (FAST), Marjorie Hobby, Harry Holmes, Malcolm Hook, Don Jones, Stuart Leslie, Alec and Elizabeth Lumsden, Stuart Marshall, Dick Richardson and Don Upward (Southampton Hall of Aviation).

Two ladies in particular warrant a special mention and my enormous thanks, Lorraine Dodd who, having bravely agreed to undertake the word processing task, has had to interpret my (occasionally) appalling handwriting – and my wife Thelma, for her patience in proof reading my text and (occasionally) nudging it in the right direction.

Photo Credits:    Fawley Historians FH
Fawley Historians/Peter New Collection FH/PNC
BAE Systems Heritage BSH
Farnborough Air Sciences Trust FAST
Alan Brown AB
Christopher Balfour CB
Stuart Leslie SL
Southampton Hall of Aviation SHA
Dick Richardson DR
Mike Phipp MP
Museum of Army Flying MAF
Southampton International Airport SIA
Blackbushe International Airport BIA
Farnborough Aircraft FA
Alec Lumsden AL
Author's Collection AC

# Introduction

Had the county boundary changes enacted in 1974 not been made, the task of compiling this book would have been much greater. As it is, with Bournemouth and Christchurch now well settled in Dorset and the Isle of Wight having 'won its independence', the gaps they have left have allowed some expansion of the aerial activities experienced within the Hampshire we know today (the aviation activites associated with these areas are expanded upon in *In Dorset's Skies* and *Saunders Roe*. Both volumes are currently available within the *Images of Aviation* series).

Nevertheless, the wealth of material that can be drawn upon is truly formidable and with so many fascinating facts and photographs regretfully having to be put aside, a residual sense of personal frustration has proved inevitable. Having said that, it is my wish that you, dear reader, will find this kaleidoscopic offering of captivating interest and that many memories will be evoked of the momentous times and events that took place over the years in Hampshire. While striving to maintain some semblance of overall chronological order, the recording of different categories that evolved concurrently made this frequently impossible. Hopefully the flow of information will not be considered to have been seriously affected.

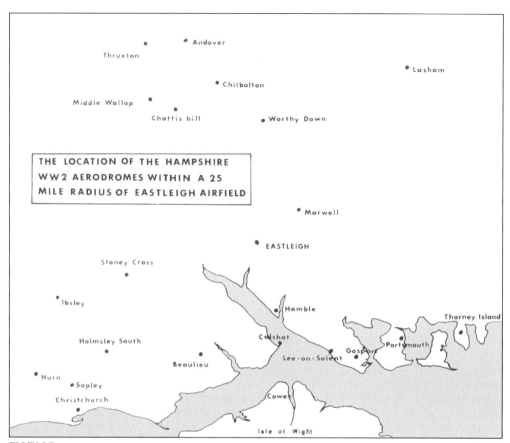

THE LOCATION OF THE HAMPSHIRE
WW2 AERODROMES WITHIN A 25
MILE RADIUS OF EASTLEIGH AIRFIELD

FH/PNC

# One

# Early Days

Throughout the nineteenth century, ballooning remained an activity enjoyed mainly by a social and sporting elite whose novel exploits have long since faded from memory. But in 1892 the Army, having already established a balloon factory at the Royal Engineers Depot at Chatham, decided to relocate it firstly, in 1892, to Aldershot and later, with more advanced airship operations in mind, to the wider spaces available at nearby Farnborough. By 1908, the Army also had its first 'heavier-than-air' machine under construction and with its first flight taking place from Farnborough on 16 October, aviation had truly arrived in Hampshire – just five years after the Wright brothers' first powered hop into the skies.

Interest in the air soon gathered pace throughout the country and within the county itself. Geoffrey de Havilland, a man destined to remain at the forefront of British aviation throughout his lifetime, made his first attempts to become airborne at Seven Barrows a few miles to the north of Whitchurch in 1910. The following year he was taken on by the Army Balloon Factory at Farnborough and, when it became the Royal Aircraft Factory in 1912, he stayed on and was appointed Inspector of Aircraft a year later. Farnborough's early days will naturally be forever associated with the flamboyant ex-Texan cowboy, 'Colonel' Samuel Franklin Cody who, in 1908, became the first person to fly a manned powered aircraft in Britain. Sadly his success and influence were short-lived for he died within five years of his pioneering achievement having, by then become a naturalised British citizen. Because of the proportionately large contribution made by Farnborough to Hampshire's aviation story, a separate chapter (6) has been devoted to its subsequent activities.

Other notable Hampshire pioneers were E.H. Eggleton of Eastleigh and Eric Rowland Moon, a Southampton resident. Eggleton built a number of reasonably successful gliders, and Rowland Moon who, in flying his Moonbeam Mark II monoplane from North Stoneham Farm between 1909-1912, can with some justification claim to have founded the airport at Eastleigh which is still located on the same site. Rowland Moon went on to join the Royal Naval Air Service at the outbreak of the First World War, serving initially at coastal stations including Calshot and later, Africa. Having survived the war years, Sqdn Ldr Moon sadly met his end along with three other crew members when his aircraft became unmanageable and spun into the sea during a routine training flight.

Another local character in this early period was the highly eccentric Noel Pemberton-Billing. He set up a company at Woolston on the River Itchen in 1913 with Hubert Scott-Paine to produce marine aircraft. The company was formally incorporated as Pemberton-Billing Ltd in 1914, but within two years it was renamed the Supermarine Aviation Works Ltd. Perhaps of more importance, it was also the year that Reginald J. Mitchell, later to become world famous for the Schneider Trophy winning seaplane and Spitfire designs, joined the firm.

In a bid to promote public interest in flying in 1910, the *Daily Mail* offered a prize of £10,000 to the winner of a London to Manchester air race. Although the winner was a Frenchman, Louis Paulhan, it was Hampshire-born Claude Grahame-White who won the hero's accolades for being the first aviator to attempt a night flight in this country. Despite losing the race, Grahame-White went on to capitalise on his flying skills, receiving the sum of $50,000 through appearing at just one airshow in Boston, USA. He used this to buy land at Hendon in North London and thus founded the famous aerodrome that staged impressive air displays throughout the 1920s and 1930s.

Grahame-White's enthusiasm for flying encouraged him to undertake two strenuous tours; one of which, along the south coast, included visiting 121 towns, giving 500 exhibition flights and carrying some 1,200 passengers. Spectators at Southampton and the Isle of Wight were no doubt inspired by the slogan 'Wake Up England' emblazoned on the side of his aircraft. This was truly the forerunner of the air circus tours carried out by Alan Cobham and other joy-riding exponents in the years following the First World War.

As the public's curiosity grew, flying schools and clubs of varying quality began to appear throughout the land. In Hampshire, Messrs Drexel and McArdle formed the New Forest flying School at Beaulieu which unfortunately lasted for barely three years, and in 1910 the Hampshire Aero Club built and flew a biplane glider at Gosport. It was also in that year that an International Air Meet took place at Southbourne (Bournemouth) then located in Hampshire. The Hon. C.S. Rolls met his untimely death at this event, which saw the biggest congregation of flying machines and personalities yet gathered together in the country. Attending the meet was Lanoe G. Hawker who, born in the Hampshire village of Longparish, was to become the first Royal Flying Corps ace, winning the VC and DSO before falling to the guns of Baron von Richthofen on 25 November 1916.

Another popular aviator and occasional visitor to Hampshire was Gustav Hamel, who had already become famous for carrying the first airmail in Britain from Hendon to Windsor in ten minutes flat. Sadly he too lost his life soon afterwards when, in 1913, he disappeared over the English Channel in dense fog.

In 1914, the naval review at Spithead included over 200 ships and an impressive flypast of thirty-eight aircraft with a supporting cast of four dirigibles (navigable airships). Although the airborne element stole the show, the imminent threat of war curtailed King George V's visit. The nation's aviation companies were now called upon to concentrate on aircraft suitable for military use and with the fighting in the air taking its toll on young lives in France and the loss of civilian lives in bombing raids on Britain, the aeroplane rapidly assumed a more sinister public image. The early days were over.

This picture, taken at HM Balloon Factory *c*.1906, suggests that the occupant of the basket may be at risk of a rapid descent. (FH/PNC)

In 1910 the military airship *Beta*, flying from Farnborough, made several flights over southern Hampshire. (FH/PNC)

Geoffrey de Havilland (1882-1965) in 1910. (AC)

De Havilland, after faltering attempts in 1909, finally got truly airborne in his second aeroplane shown here at Seven Barrows, on 10 September 1910. (BSH)

Samuel Franklin Cody (1861-1913) carried out the first officially recognised aeroplane flight in Great Britain at Farnborough on 16 October 1908. (FH/PNC)

Cody lifts off from Farnborough in his British Army Aeroplane No.3. He died along with his passenger, Hampshire cricketer W.H.B. Evans, when the aircraft he was testing crashed on 7 August 1913. (FH/PNC)

E.H. Eggleton built eleven gliders prior to the outbreak of war in 1914. Here, one of his machines leaves the ground at North End, Eastleigh, in 1913. (FH/PNC)

Eric Rowland Moon was perhaps Hampshire's best known aviator prior to the First World War. He is shown here seated under the wings of his Moonbeam 1 at Websters Field, Fawley. (FH/PNC)

Between the years 1910 and 1912 Moon achieved more success with Moonbeam 2, using the meadows at North Stoneham Farm, Eastleigh. (FH/PNC)

Shown here as a Flight Sub-Lieutenant in the Royal Naval Air Service, E.R. Moon survived active service throughout the First World War, only to perish, in April 1920, in a flying boat crash off Felixstowe, where he was Commanding Officer of the Experimental Seaplane Base. (FH/PNC)

In 1913, Noel Pemberton-Billing decided to construct boats that would fly rather than simply aeroplanes with floats. Accordingly he formed Pemberton-Billing Ltd to build the 'Supermarine' flying lifeboat. (FH/PNC)

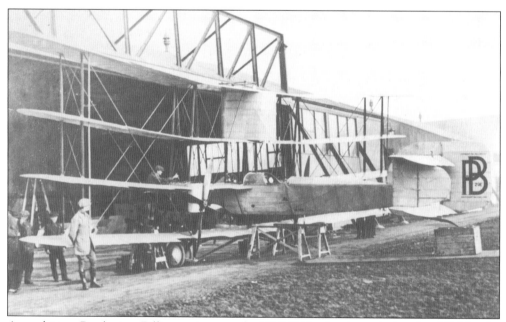

An ambitious Pemberton-Billing project was the PB 29E Quadruplane, designed in 1916 for the interception of German airships

# PEMBERTON-BILLING, Ltd.

IN FLIGHT

ILLUSTRATIONS DEMONSTRATING THE LATEST TYPE OF

# "SUPERMARINE"

### (FLYING LIFEBOAT)

*Telephone: No. 38, Southampton.*    *Telegrams: "Supermarine."*

### BUILT UNDER PEMBERTON-BILLING'S PATENTS AT HIS SOUTHAMPTON WORKS

AFTER ALIGHTING— THE WINGS DETACHED

# SOUTHAMPTON, ENGLAND

Pemberton-Billing's highly innovative approach to aircraft design was reflected in his descriptive advertising. The clever choice of 'Supermarine' in the company's telegraphic address appropriately expressed his aim to build the antithesis of the submarine. (SHA)

Pemberton-Billing's designs frequently featured the circular-section pod fuselage and pusher engine configuration as shown in the PB25 Scout (top) and Admiralty Navyplane. (SHA)

18

Reginald J. Mitchell, who joined the Supermarine Aviation Works Ltd in 1916, later achieved legendary status as its chief designer. (FH)

Claude Grahame-White won national acclaim when, in an attempt to overtake his French race rival Louis Paulhan, he became the first to fly in Britain during the hours of darkness. Prior to the start of the London-Manchester flight he received a telegram from 2,000 Hampshire residents bearing the message 'Good Luck Grahame-White, England Forever.' (FH/PNC)

Advert for the New Forest Aviation School.
(courtesy: "Flight").

NEW FOREST AVIATION SCHOOL. This was commenced at East Boldre by McArdle and Drexel in May 1910, but its active life only lasted from September 1910 to February 1911. They had successfully trained about half a dozen pilots during this period. The next major happening was at Calshot.

Armstrong Drexel & William McArdle with the manager of their Aviation School, Harry Delacombe in the centre. (courtesy: "Aero").

Armstrong Drexel (left) and William McArdle were the first to set up a flying school in the county. Manager Harry Delacombe is shown in the centre. (FH)

McArdle's 'overnight bag' could possibly have provided a weight problem for his lightly powered machine! (AC)

The New Forest Aviation School at Beaulieu, East Boldre, albeit short-lived, boasted a number of Blériot monoplanes similar to the Type XI that first flew over the channel on 25 July 1909. McArdle and his dog are on the left. (AB))

Winston Churchill, then First Lord of the Admiralty, had his first take-off from water at Calshot on 28 August 1913 and is said to have coined the word 'seaplane'. T.O.M. Sopwith is standing on the float of Churchill's mount, Maurice Farman Seaplane No.95. (FH/PNC)

1912 and 1913 saw aerial tours and exhibitions sponsored by *The Daily Mail*. M. Salmet created great interest when he landed on Southampton Common before a crowd estimated at 30,000 to 40,000 spectators on 21 August 1912. (AC)

A highlight of 1913 was *The Daily Mail* Round Britain Waterplane Race which started from Netley on 25 August. Having on his first attempt retired with sunstroke, Mr Harry Hawker flying a Sopwith seaplane covered a distance of 1,000 miles which, though failing to complete the course, was thought to be a considerable achievement. However, with no-one else finishing the race the competition was abandoned for that year. (FH)

Play came to a halt in a cricket match between Hampshire and Leicestershire when Gustav Hamel gave a particularly impressive display of aerobatics near the county ground. (SL)

Lord Grosvenor is worthy of a note in Hampshire's chronicles of early aviation. He resided at Eaglehurst Castle, Calshot, and was host on occasions to Hamel. The intrepid Lord owned a Blériot monoplane that, unusually, sported a rifle equipped with telescopic sight fixed to the side of the fuselage. (FH/PNC)

STRIKING SCENE AT SPITHEAD. AIRCRAFT OVER THE FLEET. S.CRIBB.

This striking montage was intended to impress upon a willing public the mighty strength of Britain's naval and air forces as war approached. (FH)

# Two

# The Companies Gather Pace

In addition to the unique developments that took place at Farnborough's Royal Aircraft Factory (later Establishment) a large part of the rapid growth that took place in the embryonic aircraft industry was located in Hampshire. Several major constructors either conducted their main operations or started up subsidiary activities within the county during the war and inter-war years. Today however, with the notable exceptions of Portsmouth Aviation, Aerostructures Hamble Ltd and most promisingly, Richard Noble's new Farnborough Aircraft venture, no large-scale aerospace manufacturing is carried out within the area.

Supermarine Aviation, arguably the company most famously associated with the Hampshire area, was taken over by Vickers (Aviation) Ltd in November 1928, but by then, and with R J Mitchell firmly in charge of design, the firm's success had already become well established.

Following the German air attack on Woolston in 1940, Vickers-Armstrong Supermarine moved its headquarters to Hursley Park, a large country house near Winchester and extended its operations within the county when, just after the end of the Second World War it took over Chilbolton airfield for flight test activities. Although many other local firms were engaged on component and sub-assembly work for the Spitfire, final assembly took place mainly at Castle Bromwich near Birmingham and at Eastleigh.

During the First World War the Avro, Sopwith and Fairey companies each set up aircraft assembly facilities in the Hamble area and the Gosport Aircraft Co. at Gosport along with the Camper & Nicholson boatyard at Northam, also became engaged in flying boat construction. The rather quaintly named Canute Aeroplane Co., formed as war began from the Moonbeam Co., was one of nine firms within a twenty mile radius of Southampton (including two on the Isle of Wight). They were heavily involved in wartime aircraft production but had to face the drastic cut-backs in orders when peace was restored. Avro's Gosport factory also closed in the late 1920s but Fairey's presence at Hamble, albeit later concentrated on marine products, continued beyond the Second World War. Airspeed transferred its operations from York to Portsmouth in the spring of 1933, with the first flight of its Courier monoplane taking place shortly afterwards, on 11 April. Well known for its Oxford trainer, Horsa glider and ultimately the Ambassador airliner, the company became the Airspeed Division of the de Havilland Aircraft Co. in 1951 before this famous firm was, in turn, absorbed into the Hawker Siddeley Aviation group in 1960. In 1935, British Marine Aircraft Ltd was created at Hamble to build the American Sikorsky S42A flying boat under licence. After this arrangement fell through, the company was reorganised as Folland Aircraft two years later under the leadership of H.P. Folland, formerly chief designer of the Gloster Aircraft Co. But, as with so many other leading companies, Folland's own identity disappeared following the general restructuring of Britain's aircraft industry at the end of the 1950s.

Other Hampshire based companies which flourished during that halcyon pre-war period of aircraft production were Simmonds Aircraft Ltd of Southampton, Cunliffe-Owen Aircraft Ltd, Foster Wikner Aircraft Ltd, Kay Gyroplane and the Cierva Autogiro Co. all located at Eastleigh. In addition, Air Service Training, based at Hamble was to become the country's largest wartime fighter repair facility before becoming an internationally recognised centre for civil aircrew training in the post-war years. In the late 1950s, members of the Hampshire Aeroplane Club built two light biplanes known as the Currie Wot and a twin-engined machine called the Halycon but neither went into production.

Today, great hopes for resurgence in local aircraft manufacture are being placed with Richard Noble's Farnborough Aircraft Co. This is a new organisation, set up at Farnborough to design and produce the Farnborough F1 – the first of a new generation of long-range taxi aircraft that, having a range of 1,000 miles, will provide an internet-driven on demand, point-to-point service.

Designed to provide a range of power plant and seating configurations, only one Aerocar, powered by 155hp Blackburn Cirrus Majors, finally took to the air. Today, Portsmouth Aviation produces a range of commercial and military stores loading equipment. (CB)

Portsmouth, Southsea & Isle of Wight Aviation, which undertook repair and parts manufacture during the early part of the Second World War, was re-structured as Portsmouth Aviation in 1943. Its first and only aircraft design was the Aerocar which first flew on 18 June 1947. Here, test pilot Alan Jones and passenger Peter Masefield prepare to depart from Portsmouth aerodrome. (CB)

Portsmouth Aviation's high hopes for the future are shown in this picture taken at the first SBAC Exhibition to be held at Farnborough in 1948. (CB)

Supermarine's Works at Woolston on the River Itchen in the late 1930s. Note the Walrus II on the slipway. (FH)

Supermarine took over a large hangar at Hythe when more factory floor space was required for Southampton flying boat production in the mid-1920s. This picture, taken in the late 1930s, shows a Short 'C' Class flying boat and a Sikorsky S-42A on the water. (FH)

A Supermarine Southampton II cruises over the Solent. This was the RAF's standard flying boat for the decade spanning 1925 to 1935. It also served with the Royal Australian Air Force and the Japanese and Argentinian Navies. (FH)

Vickers Vildebeest G-ABGE (fitted with Supermarine floats) was first flown from Hythe in June 1930 by Henri Biard, chief test pilot of Supermarine. (FH/PNC)

This illustration of the Supermarine Stranraer is a good example of the evocative style of advertising used by aircraft constructors in the 1930s. (FH)

Supermarine's Air Yacht of 1931 displays its elegant lines while moored in the Solent. The three-engined monoplane configuration was an unusual departure from R.J. Mitchell's more conventional twin power plant biplane layout. (FH/PNC)

The Supermarine Scapa equipped several flying boat squadrons replacing the Southampton and Fairey IIID and IIIF floatplanes until it was declared obsolete in 1939. K4192 was the second production aircraft. (FH)

A Stranraer under construction at Hythe in the mind 1930s. The F7/30 Spitfire mock-up suspended from the hangar roof provides an interesting comparison. (FH)

A Spitfire I fuselage production line typical of those to be seen at Southampton's Woolston Works and at Eastleigh. The lack of workers and any sense of urgency suggest a pre-war setting. (FH/PNC)

Spitfire prototype K5054 poses in front of an Eastleigh hangar in 1936. (FH/PNC)

Sporting its distinctive pale blue colour scheme, K5054 undergoes an early test flight over Hampshire in March 1936. Delivered to the RAF on 23 October 1937, it crashed at Farnborough on 4 September 1939, killing its pilot Flt Lt G.S. White. (FH/PNC)

Hursley Park became Vickers Supermarine's design headquarters following the Luftwaffe bombing attack on 26 September 1940. (SHA)

Jeffrey Quill took over as Supermarine's chief test pilot after George Pickering's death on 2 June 1943. (AC)

Originally called the Seagull and aimed as a private venture for the Royal Australian Air Force, the Walrus was eventually produced by Supermarine (285) and Saunders-Roe (461). Walrus hulls were constructed in a new factory a short distance from the Woolston Works and towed over to Hythe for final assembly and production tests. (FH/PNC)

Supermarine's first jet-powered design was the E1/44 which, powered by the 3,000lb thrust Rolls-Royce Nene, became the Attacker. Flying from Supermarine's flight test base at Chilbolton, Hampshire, Mike Lithgow reached 902km/hr (560.63mph) to capture the 100km Closed Circuit Record on 26 February 1948. A total of 185 Attackers were produced including thirty-six for the Pakistan Air Force. (FH)

Built at Hursley Park, VV106 was one of two prototypes ordered to investigate aerodynamic and general handling behaviour with wings and tailplane swept back by forty degrees. Initially designated Type 510, this machine soon became known as the Swift. On 8 November 1950, VV106, flown by Lt J. Elliot RN, became the first swept-winged aircraft to land on and take off from an aircraft carrier (HMS *Illustrious*). (AC)

VV119 as Supermarine Type 528, retained the tailwheel undercarriage arrangement of the Attacker and VV106. However, following extensive modifications including the fitting of a nose wheel undercarriage, it emerged as Type 535. When it later appeared in the film *Sound Barrier* as the *Prometheus* it was flown by test pilot Dave Morgan. A total of 193 production variant Swifts were built along with four prototypes and on 26 September 1953 it was a Swift Mk4 that achieved the World Absolute Speed Record of 735.7mph. (FH)

The Scimitar was the last type to be designed and built entirely within the Supermarine division of Vickers-Armstrong. Conceived initially to land onto an aircraft carrier using a shock absorbing 'carpet', the Scimitar eventually embodied a conventional undercarriage and employed 'flap-blowing' to reduce landing speed. A total of eighty-two Scimitars were built including the prototype shown here. (FH)

Avro designed and produced many varied types at its Hamble factory, several, e.g Gosport, Andover and the Aldershot (second prototype pictured here) reflecting their Hampshire town associations. (BSH)

Avro's Hamble-based factory was built when, following expanded orders for the 504 and other types, the Manchester firm's floor space proved insufficient. (SHA)

The Avro 554 Antarctic Baby, built at Hamble in 1921, was used for survey work on the Shackleton-Rowett South Polar Expedition. (BSH)

The Fairey Aviation Co. was registered in July 1915, its main factory located at Hayes, Middlesex. The following year, the Admiralty made a site available at Hamble for seaplane assembly and testing. (FH/PNC)

Based on the Sopwith Baby, the Fairey Hamble Baby featuring redesigned wings, was built largely by George Parnall & Sons at Bristol and at the Hayes factory. (FH)

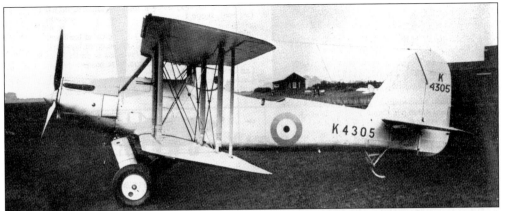

Fairey built twelve Short 827 seaplanes which were tested at Hamble before concentrating on its own products. Shown here is a later design, the second prototype Fairey Sea Fox at Hamble, 5 November 1937. Total production reached sixty-four between 1937 and 1938. (AC)

Perhaps more easily identified without its 'sea boots' was the Fairey Swordfish, which sank more enemy tonnage in the Second World War than any other type of Allied aircraft. Total Swordfish production was 2,392 (1,700 manufactured by Blackburn Aircraft) with testing of the float plane variant being carried out at Hamble. (FH)

The Gosport Aircraft Co. built and assembled Felixstowe-designed flying boats throughout the First World War. (FH/PNC)

In March 1932 Airspeed Ltd moved from York to Portsmouth. The first machine produced at the Hampshire factory was the Airspeed Courier, which, despite the general upheaval, first flew the following month. (AC)

The Airspeed Envoy gave rise to a series of derivatives that included the Oxford trainer, the Consul, and the Viceroy light transport aircraft. (AC)

George Errington was Airspeed's chief test pilot until he was killed in a Trident crash in June 1966. (BSH)

Harry Folland (second from left) ever the dandy with a team of Gloster executives. Folland Aircraft was formed in 1937 on a Hamble site covering 120 acres. (AC)

Attempts by Folland to promote the Gnat as an ultra-lightweight fighter were largely unsuccessful. The Gnat however, proved its mettle as an advanced pilot training machine until replaced by the BAe Hawk in the late 1970s. (FH/PNC)

Simmonds Aircraft produced its first machine in 1928. Designed by Oliver Simmonds, the first chairman of the Hampshire Aero Club, the Spartan sporting biplane was considered by many to be the equal of the ubiquitous DH Moth, Avro Avian and Blackburn Bluebird. (SHA)

Geoffrey N. Wikner, an Australian gliding pioneer, set up a company at Eastleigh in 1937 with Messrs Foster and Lusty. The Foster Wikner Wicko proved popular with aero clubs and a number of these were impressed for RAF communications work during the Second World War. (SHA)

Cunliffe-Owen Aircraft Co., the largest single firm to occupy factory space at Eastleigh, produced its revolutionary twin-boom flying wing in 1939. Originally destined to join Olley Air Services for the London-Dublin service, the concept was overtaken by the Second World War. In 1941 this distinctive machine was ferried by the well-known aviator Jim Mollison to West Africa for use by the Free French Air Force. (FH/PNC)

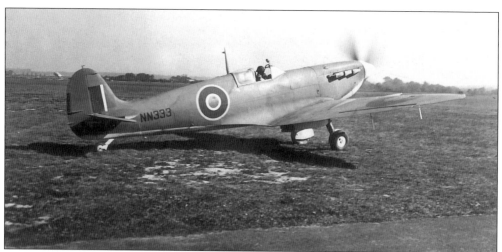

Some 400 Seafire IIIs were assembled by Cunliffe-Owen at Eastleigh during the Second World War. (SHA)

Cunliffe-Owen's wartime activity at Eastleigh and Swaythling included servicing, modification and special installation work on a large variety of British and American aircraft such as the Bell P.39 Airacobra shown here. The Airacobra saw limited service with the RAF, most machines being sent to Russia. (SHA)

The Concordia was a twelve-seat feeder airliner for which Cunliffe-Owen saw bright prospects in the immediate post-war period. The prototype, powered by a 550hp Alvis Leonides engines, flew from Eastleigh on 19 May 1947, but failed to impress the airlines. (SHA)

Kay Gyroplanes, formed at Eastleigh in 1929, produced its first successful autogyro in 1932. This is the Gyroplane, built in 1935. (FH)

The Cierva Autogyro Co. granted construction licences to several companies, one of which was Avro who built the machines at Hamble. Shown here is the Cierva C9 (Avro Type 576) fitted with a 70hp Genet radial engine faired into the square-section fuselage. It was first flown by Avro test pilot H.J. 'Bert' Hinkler in September 1927. (AC)

The impressive Cierva WII Air Horse was Britain's largest helicopter with three rotors driven from a single 1,620 hp Rolls Royce Merlin engine. Prototype G-ALCV first flew at Eastleigh on 7 December 1948, but crashed on 13 June 1950 killing the crew. (FH)

Alongside the Air Horse are Alan Marsh, (chief test pilot), Dr Shapiro (chief designer), Basil Arkell (test pilot) and Joe Unsworth (flight engineer). (FH/PNC)

G-ADSR, the first of twelve Ensigns for Imperial Airways took to the air for its maiden flight on 24 January 1938. (AC)

Owing to heavy commitments for the Royal Air Force, Armstrong Whitworth Aircraft was obliged to find a facility outside its Whitley factory for the production of the Ensign airliner. Accordingly a lease was obtained from Air Service Training (another member of the Hawker Siddeley group) for the use of the Hamble workshops. Here the second Ensign, G-ADSS, emerges from the flight shed for its first engine runs. (AL)

# *Three*

# Civil Operations

Hampshire's long association with aviation has seen many of its airfields alternate between civil and military use and although this chapter attempts to dwell on the development of the former, pictorial separation, particularly in the case of Blackbushe and Southampton, has not been strictly adhered to. Perhaps the most glamorous airline operations to be linked with the county were the major over-water routes flown by Imperial Airways, British Overseas Airways Corporation, Pan American Airways and Air France. In both pre- and post-war years the large flying boats belonging to these companies flew from Southampton and used the Hythe terminal for servicing, repairs and maintenance.

Many other concerns have also served the continent and elsewhere over many years and, though Portsmouth Airport finally closed its hangar doors in 1973, Blackbushe remains a thriving modern business with two flying schools, executive charter flights and a large number of private owners flying from the Airport. Southampton International Airport as the name suggests, is fully engaged in general aviation and airline operations, while Farnborough, though best known to the public for hosting the SBAC flying displays, is also home to executive charter and light aircraft organisations.

Today, Lasham, not only provides baseline maintenance facilities for large aircraft, but also serves as a major UK centre for gliding enthusiasts. Still at the lighter end of the aviation scale, Thruxton and Popham airfields remain amongst the most popular recreational flying venues in the south of England.

Three Supermarine Sea Eagles were built for the British Marine Air Navigation Company to operate between Southampton and Cherbourg, Le Havre and the Channel Islands. The first flew in June 1923. Shown here is the third machine G-EBGS in front of the Woolston 'Marine Airport'. On 31 March 1924, BMAN along with other private airlines, became part of Imperial Airways, which was formed by the government to develop British commercial aviation. (FH)

Providing an interesting contrast to R.J. Mitchell's flying boat design, is this Dornier Wal (Whale), similar to the machine that on a Swedish airline proving flight, visited the Imperial Airways station at Woolston in 1925. (FH)

Imperial Airways operated the Short Calcutta between Southampton and Guernsey between 1928-1929 and later, three were handed over to Imperial's Air Service Training Limited as conversion trainers for the 'C' Class flying boats. A total of six Calcuttas were built. (AC)

Contemporary railway carriage design appears to have influenced the cabin interior of the Calcutta flying boat! (AC)

The old and the new. The 1930s saw the flying boat beginning to threaten the ocean-going liners' traditional hold on luxury travel. Imperial eventually ordered a total of twenty-eight S.23 'C' Class machines, the first (*Canopus*), undertaking its first flight on 3 July 1936. *Champion*, shown here, was the first of nine S.30 boats which offered twice the range of the S.23. Providing the nautical background at Southampton is the *Empress of Australia*. (FH)

'C' Class boat *Ceres* appears to be sporting a daunting array of radar aerials as it taxies past a tall ship in Southampton docks. (FH)

The large sheds at Hythe used by May, Harden & May during the First World War for flying boat manufacture were later used for maintenance work by Imperial and other major airlines. (FH)

A Pan American Airways Sikorsky S-42A at Hythe in rather bleak weather conditions. (FH)

The Short-Mayo Composite aircraft was considered to be an alternative means to air-to-air refuelling when trying to achieve greater range. Pictured here at Hythe, the combination was not regarded as successful and *Mercury* (i.e. the top component) was scrapped in 1941, and *Maia* was destroyed in a bombing attack on Poole Harbour the same year. (FH)

Beaching legs had to be floated out and attached to a flying boat's hull before it could be brought ashore for maintenance. (FH)

THE QUEEN MARY FROM HYTHE SHORE ROAD.

This pleasing study shows the *Queen Mary* leaving Southampton with several Imperial Airways machines about to rock in its wake. *Maia*, the Mayo Composite lower half, is in line with the *Queen's* centre funnel. (FH)

State-of-the-art American style! Pan American's Boeing 314A *Yankee Clipper* rides gently at its Hythe mooring. (FH)

And off! Maintenance complete and *Yankee Clipper* lifts off from Southampton water on the journey home. (FH)

57

The difference in national approaches to flying boat design is well illustrated in the sleek, elongated profile of this Air France Latécoère 631 F-BDRA, shown visiting Southampton on 15 July 1947. (FH)

Air France's Breguet 530 Saigon *Tunisie* was a regular continental visitor to Southampton. (FH)

Showing marked diversity of design is this Loire-et-Olivier H242-1 *Ville d'Oran*, caught high and dry at Hythe. (FH)

An Air France Loire-et-Olivier H49 (S.E.200) at rest on Southampton Water. (FH)

In the late 1930s Flight Refuelling Ltd, a company set up by Sir Alan Cobham in 1934, equipped Imperial Airways 'C' class flying boats to receive fuel from its HP Harrow tankers. A series of eight return crossings of the Atlantic carrying mail but not passengers, was successfully carried out just prior to the outbreak of the Second World War. Here, *Cabot* takes on fuel as it turns towards the Hamble River. (AC)

To offset the taking on of overload fuel in flight it was necessary to develop an emergency fuel jettison system. *Cabot*, seen here over Hythe, demonstrates its ability to dump fuel. (AC)

An atmospheric 1948 study of a Solent 2 flying over the Hythe maintenance terminal which was soon to be abandoned for Berth 50 in Southampton docks. (FH)

This picture of the first and the last flying boat types to be operated by Imperial/BOAC was taken in September 1949. The Supermarine Seagull hull is actually that of G-EBGR. The original G-EBGS was rammed and sunk by a ship in St. Peter Port harbour on 10 January 1927! *Somerset* was a Short Solent 2 G-AHIO, one of twelve produced for BOAC, capable of carrying thirty-four passengers and a crew of seven. It operated the final BOAC flying boat service into Southampton on 14 November 1951. (FH)

'With a little bit of help from my friends', i.e. launch skipper Dave Etheridge, ex-Antilles Airways Sandringham, *Southern Cross* 'flies' up the slipway at Calshot prior to ending its days in the Southampton Hall of Aviation as *Beachcomber*. (FH)

Grand finale! Britain's last flying Sunderland ML814 and latterly Antilles Airways *Islander*, now renamed *Fantasy of Flight*, prepares to leave Calshot for a new life in America, 6 July 1993. (FH)

Although defunct since 1973, Portsmouth possessed an active airport that had its official opening on 2 July 1932. At that time, the sole users were Portsmouth, Southsea & Isle of Wight Aviation (previously Wight Aviation). PSIOW eventually operated a fleet of Courier, Monospar, Wessex, Dragon and Fox Moth aircraft on its south coast services. (CB)

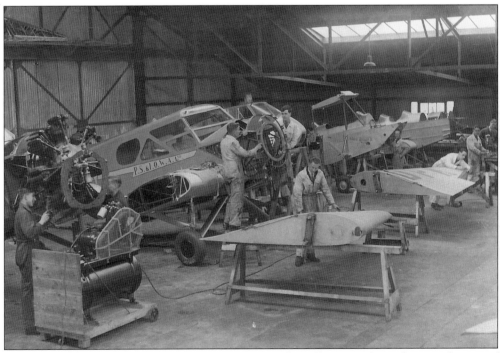

'Look busy chaps, there's a photographer about' – might well sum up this rather posed group of PSIOW workers at Portsmouth. (CB)

'Tootling along' to the Isle of Wight, PSIOW's chief pilot Charles Eckersley-Maslin gives passengers a grandstand view of Southsea's South Parade Pier from Monospar G-ABVN. (CB)

The 'big boys' put in the occasional appearance at Portsmouth. Here, an Armstrong Whitworth Argosy disgorges a load of passengers in rather casual fashion. (CB)

This contrived shot of Portsmouth airport (e.g what is the French-looking official doing there?) nevertheless shows an interesting group of aircraft. Below the Cirrus powered Klemm, are left to right, a DH60 Moth, Simmonds Spartan, DH 'Puss Moth', Westland Wessex and (foreground) a G.A Monospar. (CB)

Portsmouth Airport's close proximity to the sea is shown in this fine aerial view. Airspeed's works are in the foreground. (BSH)

Sir Alan Cobham and Courier co-pilot Sqdn Ldr Bill Helmore. (AC)

On 22 September 1934, Sir Alan Cobham attempted to fly non-stop from Portsmouth to Karachi. His first air-to-air refuelling contact was made directly after take off from a Handley Page W10. A disconnected throttle linkage later caused Cobham's Courier to force land in Malta and the record attempt was not continued. (AC)

Taken just before the closure of Portsmouth Airport, Fairchild Argus 2 G-AJPI poses for the camera on 20 May 1972. (MP)

Caught (s)napping on the same day was this Scottish Aviation Twin Pioneer 1 G-APHX belonging to J. Fisher Aviation. (MP)

What is now Blackbushe Airport first opened in January 1943 as RAF Hartfordbridge. To assist the safe landing of damaged aircraft in bad weather the airfield was also equipped with the Fog Investigation and Dispersal Operation (FIDO) system. This picture shows the layout of the airfield site, today owned by British Car Auctions. (BIA (CS Photography))

The Douglas Boston was one of many types of medium bomber that also included the Mitchell, Ventura and Mosquito, to operate from Blackbushe during the Second World War. (AC)

An interesting visitor to Blackbushe in the early 1950s was this RAF Coastal Command Handley Page Hastings. (BIA)

This pleasing shot shows an Airwork Handley Page Hermes 4A (civil, pressurised version of the Hastings) that flew from Blackbushe throughout the 1950s. (BIA)

The United States Navy occupied part of Blackbushe airfield in the 1950s. Impressive indeed is this Lockheed P2V-7 Neptune as it touches down after a long-range patrol. (BIA)

The Douglas C-54 Skymaster was widely used throughout the 1940s and 1950s by the United States forces. When production ceased in 1947 a total of 1,163 Skymasters had been built, 1,084 of these as the C-54 military transport version such as shown here at Blackbushe. (BIA)

Frequently seen at Blackbushe was the U S Navy's Lockheed R7V-1 'flying radar station'. The eight-foot vertical structure above the fuselage-housed height-finding antenna, and the lower central radome contained a bearing antenna. (BAI)

As the private registration letters would imply, this Spitfire MkXVI is shown as belonging to the Doug Arnold collection. It was previously used by ACM Sir James M. Robb as his 'personal mount' when based at Northolt. (DR)

The owner of Blackbushe airport in the 1970s was entrepreneur Doug Arnold. A very private individual, his highly prized 'warbird collection' was rarely available for public viewing. (DR)

More Arnold machines. Three two-seat Hawker Sea Fury T Mk20 operational trainers make a pretty line up at Blackbushe. (DR)

Occasionally the 'warbirds' made a welcome appearance. Seen here are a Sea Fury T20, Sopwith Pup Replica, Meteor NF11, two Harvards, Chipmunk, Auster and Tiger Moth. All of these were housed at Blackbushe. (DR)

'Powering in' at Blackbushe in the early 1970s is Lancaster PA474. The pilot is erstwhile British aerobatic champion Neil Williams. Note the absence of the top turret now a feature on the RAF's Battle of Britain Flight machine. (DR)

Showing one of three CASA 352-L machines (licence-built Junkers 52/3m) resident at Blackbushe for several years, this beautifully sharp photograph reveals a wealth of constructional detail. (DR)

Seemingly a most unlikely pair to share the Blackbushe apron; the Grimes Beech 18 'Flying Laboratory' used for evaluating strobe lighting in the wing-tip pods and the Lockheed P-80 *Black Knight* in which its owner, Ormond Haydon-Baillie later lost his life. (DR)

More in keeping with the aircraft types resident at Blackbushe today, is this Beech 400A used as a corporate jet by Air Hansen. (BIA)

A new RAF Fleet Air Arm reconditioning base was formed at Southampton Airport in 1935. Originally called RAF Eastleigh, from 1 August 1936 it became officially known as RAF Southampton. (FH/PNC)

Developed from the First World War Atlantic Park aerodrome, Southampton's Municipal Aerodrome was formally opened in 1932. For some years afterwards, it was often still referred to as Eastleigh Airport, but on 15 March 1935 it officially became Southampton Municipal Airport. Jersey Airways was one of the earliest operators to fly from the airport. Shown here is the airline's DH86 G-ACYG. (FH/PNC)

The Duke and Duchess of Kent arriving at Southampton's airport in a de Havilland Rapide in 1935. (FH/PNC)

Hawker Audaxes of Nos 4 and 13 Squadrons flew from RAF Southampton during summer camp in 1935.

Avro Ansons belonging to Nos 224 and 269 Squadrons based at RAF Southampton undertook reconnaissance patrols for Coastal Command in 1938. (AC)

On 1 July 1939, RAF Southampton was recommissioned as HMS *Raven* and subsequently spent most of the Second World War in a ground and air training role for the Royal Navy. Hawker Ospreys of Nos 800, 801, 802 and 822 Squadrons were a common sight at Southampton during the late 1930s and formed part of the early wartime airfield defence force. Following raids by the Luftwaffe, German propaganda reported that HMS *Raven* had been sunk! (AC)

Part of HMS *Raven* with an intriguingly styled vehicle guaranteed to attract attention. (SIA (FAA Museum))

Forming part of HMS *Raven's* flying element in 1940 was this Hawker Osprey (centre) and Fairey Seal. (SIA (FAA Museum))

In August 1940, a tragedy occurred when a Lockheed Hudson belonging to No.1 O.T.U took off from HMS *Raven*, only to fly into the securing cable of a barrage balloon that was being hurriedly raised in response to a 'red alert' air raid warning. Both crew members and the occupants of a house in Nutbeam Road, Eastleigh were killed in the ensuing crash. (SIA)

This 'gathering of eagles' took place at Southampton's airport in 1986 to commemorate the fiftieth anniversary of the Spitfire's first flight from this same location. (SIA)

'It takes all kinds' – as seen here with this Avro Triplane replica leaving Southampton. It was built by the Hampshire Aero Club for the film *Those Magnificent Men In Their Flying Machines*. (SIA)

Southampton's control tower sets off this neat study of a Handley Page Jetstream 31 used by Birmingham European in the 1980s. (SIA)

Air UK was the first British carrier to introduce the 100 seat BAe, 146-200 into the scheduled domestic network. The airline operated a service using this type between Guernsey and Southampton in the 1980s. (SIA)

Southampton International Airport's location adjacent to the M27 motorway makes it one of the most accessible airports in the UK. The buildings to the right of the motorway, now occupied by Ford, are on the site of the Cunliffe-Owen Aircraft factory. No buildings exist today that formed HMS *Raven*, once located on the far (eastern) side of the runway. (SIA)

The closeness of Southampton's airport to major sea, rail and road links provides advantages enjoyed by few other regional organisations. Shown here is the main terminal and administration area. (SIA)

The scrapman cometh! This sad sight at Lasham shows dismembered Canadian Sabre 6 front fuselages awaiting their final journey in May 1963. (MP)

From 1953 to the mid-1960s, Dan-Air Services of London operated a mixed business of short-haul scheduled services, inclusive tour charters and miscellaneous freight operations using machines such as this ex-RAF Transport Command Avro York at Lasham. (BIA)

By far the most extensive user of Comets from the mid-1960s, Dan Air purchased forty-eight of the various types (series 4, 4B and 4C) though only about a third of this number were in use at any given time. Shown here at Lasham, where it was scrapped in October 1978 is Comet 4C-G-AROV. (MP)

Lasham is today owned, appropriately enough, by the Lasham Gliding Club which was formed in 1950. Shown here awaiting some action at a vintage glider meet in August 1986 is a Slingsby Cadet 3 T31. (MP)

Popham airfield is privately owned and operated by Charles Church Spitfires Ltd. Originally created out of light woodland by Jim Espin, Popham held its first 'fly in' in 1978. Purchased by the late Charles Church in 1988, Popham is today a highly popular centre for events such as the Microlight Trade Fair shown here in 1995. (DR (Roger D. Smith))

A typical scene at Popham. Lots of 'de Havillands' on show here, including the DH60 Gipsy Moth, nearest camera. (MP)

Well look who's here! Touching down in Popham's delightful rural setting is Vimy replica G-EAOU. (DR)

Bringing a distinctly eastern European flavour to the light aircraft scene at Popham is this Russian built Technovia SM-92 Finist, which arrived in Spring 1995 for a UK sales tour. Mythology claims the Finist to have been a bird that became transformed into a prince! (DR)

# Four

# Military Miscellany

Hampshire's location in the centre of Britain's south coast automatically placed it in the operational front-line in both the First and Second World Wars.

Between 1912 and 1939, the following Royal Flying Corps, Royal Naval Air Service and Royal Air Force stations were brought into service in Hampshire; Gosport (1912), Calshot (1913), Hamble (1914), Chattis Hill (1914), Beaulieu, East Boldre (1915), Worthy Down (1917), Lee-on-Solent (1917), Andover (1917), Lopcombe Corner (1917), Portsmouth (1924), Middle Wallop (1935), Odiham (1936) and Chilbolton (1939).

Already used by a number of aviators in the years prior to the First World War, the meadowland between Swaythling and Eastleigh was soon earmarked for military use in 1914. Eastleigh's contribution to the war effort gained extra importance when, following the arrival of American forces in Europe, it was chosen by the US Navy Air Force to become a major repair site for its Northern Bombing Group aircraft.

During the Second World War, Thruxton, Blackbushe, Ibsley, Lasham, Holmsley South, Marwell and Stoney Cross also became operational as main or satellite bases. In addition, Winkton, Bisterne, Lymington and Needs Oar Point (although sometimes referred to as Needs Ore Point, Needs Oar Point was the official RAF description) were also brought into temporary use as advanced landing grounds in the period leading up to the Allied invasion of France. Quite a formidable list for one county and to that number of wartime bases could be added Hurn and Christchurch, both now located firmly 'over the border.'

The Farman Longhorn was used for training at Gosport before the arrival of the more renowned Avro 504. (FH)

A coastal station at Gosport was already established before the First World War. This picture shows Avro 504J, B3157, which, following the installation of the 130hp Clerget engine, made this the first 'K' variant. (SL)

Not so fortunate was this Gosport-based Avro 504A which crashed on 29 April 1917. (SL)

This picture shows not only a Sopwith Camel B.5157 of 'F' Flight, School of Special Flying but an interesting attempt to camouflage the Gosport buildings with a turf covering. (SL)

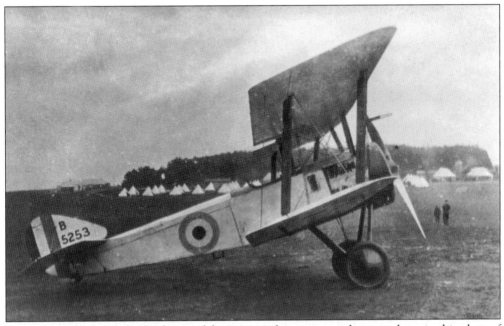

Another example of the background being as informative as the aeroplane is this shot of Lopcombe Corner, showing No.3 Training Depot Squadron's tented accommodation and a Sopwith Pup, B.5253 *c.* 1917. (SL)

Established in 1917, Lee-on-Solent became home to No.209 Training Depot Squadron's Sopwith 320's, seen here moored along the shoreline. In later years, after the Second World War, the Fleet Air Arm maintenance unit at Fleetlands used Lee-on-Solent as its test airfield. (SL)

Eastleigh saw the arrival of American personnel in early 1918 when it formed a repair and maintenance base at Wide Lane. DH4, DH6 and DH9a day and night bombers were delivered by the US Navy Air Force to Ingleverte in France for the 10th Bombing Group. (FH/PNC)

Beaulieu (East Boldre), having already served as the New Forest Flying School in 1910-1912, was re-activated as the Royal Flying Corp's flying training base in 1915. Shown here is one of four hangars constructed near the Beaulieu-Lymington road. (AB)

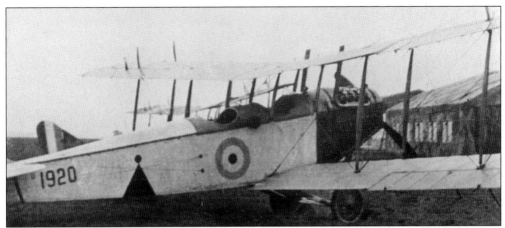

One of the aircraft used by No.16 Reserve School at Beaulieu was this Curtiss JN4A pictured in 1917. Other types based there included SE5s, DH9 and Sopwith Dolphins. (SL)

The Hawker Audax was an Army Co-operation aircraft used in large numbers during the many training maneouvres held in southern Hampshire during the 1930s. (FH/PNC)

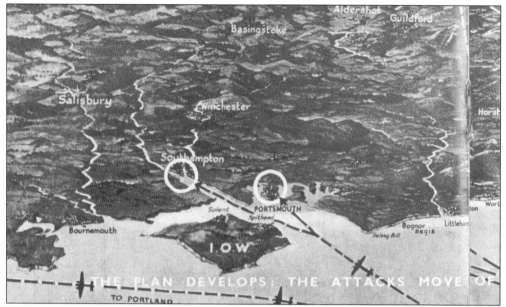

As the Battle of Britain reached its peak during Phase 2 (19 August - 5 September 1940), prime targets for the Luftwaffe bomber fleets included Hampshire's port cities, Portsmouth and Southampton. (FH/PNC)

Middle Wallop's No.604 Squadron Blenheim and Beaufighter night fighter crews included Wg Cdr John Cunningham and Plt Off. C. F. 'Jimmy' Rawnsley. Here, Cunningham meets HM King George VI in the mess at Middle Wallop on 7 May 1941. (MAF)

RAF Middle Wallop suffered several air attacks, the heaviest being on 14 August 1940 when a Ju88 brought about a rapid end to this Blenheim's flying days. Two more Blenheims and three Spitfires were destroyed and three civilian workmen killed in this raid. (MAF)

Mustang Is of No.16 Squadron based at Middle Wallop provided close ground support for the Army. Here Flg Off. D.W. Sampson and ground crew confer on 3 June 1943. (SHA)

Middle Wallop is now the home of the Army Air Corps which, in 2002, celebrates the forty-fifth anniversary of its founding. Symbolising the Army's use of the helicopter is this Eurocopter (Aerospatiale) SA341 Gazelle, which first flew in 1967. (MAF)

Heinkel 115 float planes were flown by Norwegian crews to England, where, after modifications at BOAC's maintenance base at Hythe, they were used by the RAF, operating from Calshot, to deliver and pick up secret agents along enemy coastlines and inland waters. (FH)

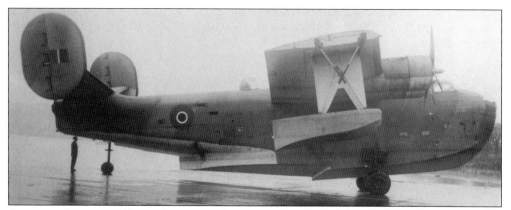

An unusual visitor to Britain's wartime shores was this Consolidated Coronado which served with RAF Coastal Command at Calshot. (FH)

Sunderland city! Note the flying control watch office on top of Calshot's castle. (FH)

Although not widely used by the RAF in Britain, the Curtiss Tomahawk operated with No.400 Squadron from RAF Odiham. (SHA)

Ibsley 1941 and some of the Sergeant pilots of No.118 Squadron, one of several that flew Spitfires from this Hampshire airfield during the Second World War. Ibsley was originally constructed as a satellite airfield for Middle Wallop. It was also used to provide the flying sequences in the wartime film *First of the Few*, that featured Leslie Howard. (SHA)

A familiar sight in southern skies during 1943-1944 were the RAF's 2nd Tactical Air Force Typhoon fighter-bombers flying from Bealieu and Holmsley South in the New Forest. (FH/PNC)

2nd Tactical Air Force also operated two squadrons of Tempest V fighters from Chilbolton just prior to the invasion of Europe. (FH/PNC)

RAF Beaulieu opened in 1942 and closed in 1950. During that period it was used by RAF Coastal Command Halifaxes and Liberators, and 9th US AAF Thunderbolts and Marauders. In 1944 it became home to the Airborne Forces Experimental Establishment. Here, an AFEE Valetta tows off a Horsa glider. (AC)

An interesting mix is provided by the Airspeed Ambassador, Beaufighter TTX and Harvards at Beaulieu just prior to its closure in 1950. In 1953, repairs were undetaken that brought the airfield up to standby base status for possible use by the US Air Force. However, never used by the Americans, it went on to a care and maintenance basis for the final time in 1956. (BSH)

RAF Stoney Cross had a relatively short operational life between 1943 and 1946. From November 1944 until its closure, RAF Transport Command's Nos 46 and 242 Squadrons operated Stirling Vs, (shown here), Yorks and Dakotas. (AB)

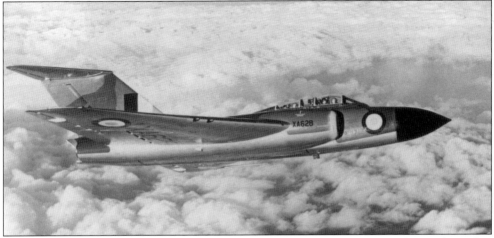

In the 1950s, No.46 Squadron was equipped with the Gloster Javelin F(AW)Mk1 all-weather fighter and based at Odiham. (BSH)

Seen here lined up for the 1953 Coronation Royal Review are Odiham's Vampires and B.29 Washingtons. Despite the presence of a Second World War-vintage balloon, it is not thought an enemy attack was imminent! (BSH)

These two squadrons of Canberras were just part of the massive fly-past of aircraft that took place at Odiham during the Royal Review. (AC)

# Five

# Calshot and the Schneider Trophy Races

Undoubtedly the most popular association the aviation enthusiast has of Calshot is that of the Schneider Trophy races held there in 1929 and 1931. Capturing the public imagination in a manner perhaps unimaginable today, the Royal Air Force's High Speed Flight, along with the Supermarine and the Rolls Royce design teams – and not forgetting Lady Houston's considerable investment – overcame immense technical and financial obstacles to secure the Trophy in perpetuity for Great Britain. But Calshot's links with the air began well before this and continued long afterwards. An Admiralty flying-boat base was built on Calshot Spit in 1913 and it fulfilled this function until 1953. It also served as the RAF's main centre for marine craft from 1927 until 1961, since when, owned by Hampshire County Council, it has found a new lease of life as a sports training centre.

The 1914 Spithead Naval Review included 216 ships, 38 aircraft and 4 airships. This Short S81 No.126 Gunbus was one of the Calshot based machines that took part in the royal fly-past. (FH/PNC)

Also featured in the Naval Review was this Short Type 74 which first flew on 4 January 1914. A total of eleven Type 74 machines were delivered to the RNAS in 1914. (FH/PNC)

An early scene at Calshot with a rather dejected looking Felixstowe F2A clearly out of its element. (FH)

Much more at home on the water are these Calshot-based F2A machines normally used for coastal patrol duties. (FH)

With an F2A in the background, a Short 320 seaplane executes a wet and windy departure from Calshot in February 1918. (FH)

A notable achievement in 1927-1928 was the successful journey undertaken to Australia and back by the RAF's Calshot-based Far East Flight. Encompassing some 27,000 miles, the four Supermarine Southampton IIs led by Wing Commander Cave-Brown-Cave encountered no serious problems and the flight greatly enhanced Supermarine's reputation as a leading flying boat constructor. (FH/PNC)

The Far East Flight collected information on potential seaplane bases, harbours and local conditions to assist the opening up of Empire air routes. (FH/PNC)

Squadron Commander Arthur Longmore RN was the first airman to drop a standard fourteen-inch torpedo from a naval aircraft. This took place at Calshot on 28 July 1914. (FH)

The first of Britain's three consecutive Schneider victories was at Venice in 1927 when Flt Lt Webster, shown here with R.J. Mitchell (centre) and the Supermarine team, achieved a winning speed of 281.65mph in S5.S220. (FH)

Although he served at Calshot during te 1929 Schneider Trophy races, Aircraftsman 338171 T.E. Shaw (more famously known as Lawrence of Arabia) returned in 1931 to join the British Power Boat Co. in the development of high-speed rescue launches. He is pictured here (on the right) on Southampton Water with Hubert Scott-Paine. (FH)

On 12 March 1928, Flt Lt Sam Kinkead of the High Speed Flight, met his death when his S5, S221, dived into the Solent off Calshot Light. Kinkead, second from right, was about to make an attempt on the World Air Speed Record. (FH)

Kinkead taxies out in the ill fated machine. (FH/PNC)

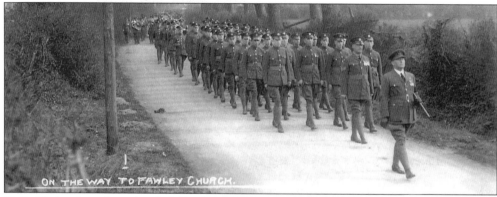

ON THE WAY TO FAWLEY CHURCH.

Flt Lt Kinkead was buried with full military honours at Fawley Church. (FH/PNC)

The floats (top) and fuselage (bottom) bear sad testimony to the force of impact. Kinkead's body at first thought to be lost, was discovered in the rear of the fuselage. (FH/PNC)

H.P. Folland's team placed its faith in his Gloster IV (shown here) and Gloster V biplane designs, but both failed to come up to expectations in the 1927 and 1929 competitions. (FH)

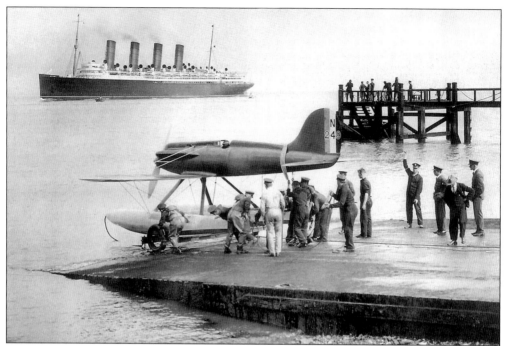

Great hopes were placed on the Gloster VI Golden Arrow, but technical snags caused the two machines built for the 1929 race, N249 and N250, to be withdrawn. The liner *Mauretania*, steaming into Southampton Water seems to be providing a rival claim for the cameraman's attention. (FH)

Gloster's Golden Arrow shows off its superb styling. It briefly held the Absolute Speed Record when, on 10 September 1929 and flown by Flt Lt George Stainforth, N249 averaged 336.3mph over the three-kilometre course at Calshot. (FH)

It was Flt Lt Waghorn flying Supermarine S6, N247, that clinched the 1929 race for Great Britain with a speed of 328.63mph. (FH)

Although they entered a strong team of Fiat C29, Savoia S65, Macchi M67 and M52R (shown here) machines, the Italians had to settle for second place in 1929. Perhaps being pictured with the Prince of Wales provided some consolation! (FH)

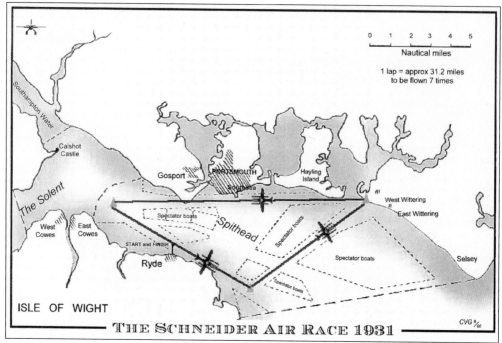

The ultimate British success came in 1931 when Flt Lt Boothman notched up an average speed of 340.08mph (over seven laps) in the Supermarine S6B over the course shown here. (FH)

Despite the previous successes, the deep national economic depression caused a loss of government financial support. It was only the timely intervention of Lady Houston who donated £100,000 that allowed the British team to compete in 1931. (FH)

## Six

# Farnborough – the Testing Years

Since the birth of flight in Great Britain, Farnborough has continued to play an active and innovative role in its development. The Royal Aircraft Factory, Royal Aircraft Establishment and today the Defence Establishment Research Association (DERA) have been and continue to be the country's 'centre of excellence' for aeronautical research. But whilst the aerospace industry has traditionally relied on Farnborough's technical expertise and professionalism to guide the way ahead, the general public and overseas visitors' impressions of Farnborough are more often associated with the equipment exhibitions and allied flying displays now promoted every two years by the Society of British Aerospace Companies. The following illustrations can, in spanning the years, merely hint at the range of activities undertaken at the place where, in the UK, military aviation first began to grow.

Following the move from Aldershot in 1905, HM Balloon factory technicians constructed the army airship *Nulli Secundus II* (shown here). It made but one long distance flight, from Farnborough to London, then on to Crystal Palace on 5 October 1907, only to be destroyed in a storm five days later. (FAST)

Other airships appearing in Farnborough's skies included the *Astra Torres*, shown here emerging from the flight shed. A second large shed can be seen under construction. (FAST)

The typically flimsy construction of the crew compartment of Farnborough's airships is well demonstrated here. Note the fuel tank suspended beneath the airship keel. At the outbreak of the First World War, the Royal Flying Corp's airships *Beta*, *Delta* and *Gamma* were turned over to the Royal Naval Air Service for coastal patrol duties. (FAST)

'Colonel' Cody looking every bit the wild west showman as Instructor in Kiting, supervises his man-lifting kite at Laffans Plain, Farnborough c.1906. (FAST)

This re-enactment of a Balloon and Kite Company of the Royal Engineers handling the Cody kite, took place at Farnborough in 1955. (FAST)

Cody's enthusiasm for flying led to his becoming the first man to pilot a heavier-than-air machine in his British Army Aeroplane No.1 on 16 October 1908. The flight at Farnborough, covered 424m (1,390 feet) and ended in a crash, fortunately without injury to Cody. (FAST)

Inevitably perhaps, Cody's luck finally ran out when he crashed on Farnborough's Ball Hill on 9 August 1913. (FAST)

Regarded as a national hero, Cody was buried with full military honours. (FAST)

Workers leaving the Royal Aircraft Factory at Farnborough in 1914. This was renamed Royal Aircraft Establishment in 1918 to avoid confusion with the Royal Air Force formed in that year. (SL)

Ahead of his time was Farnborough aerodynamicist J.W. Dunne who demonstrated the effects of sweep-back on wing design before the First World War. (FAST)

Providing a pleasing study is this RAE Coastal Experimental No.1 although everyone appears to be rather unsure what to do next! (FAST)

Posing for the cameraman at Farnborough on 16 February 1918, are the crew of a Handley Page 0/100 and the pilot of an SE5. (FAST)

As part of its technical research programme, the RAE experimented with air-to-air refuelling techniques in the 1920s and 1930s. Here, the refuelling hose trailing from the Virginia tanker's hose is about to be caught and secured by a crewman in the Virginia receiver's rear gun position. (AC)

This unusual picture shows the Bristol 142 *Britain First* in a somewhat sad state. Forerunner of the Blenheim series, this aircraft ended its days contributing to a structural research programme before its final dismantling at Farnborough. (FAST)

In August 1940, the RAE began to investigate the possibility of launching large land-based aircraft using a track and trolley system. The first aircraft to be successfully launched from what was called the Direction-Controlled, Take-Off System was this Avro Manchester at an all-up weight of 38,000lb. Note also the hook under the rear fuselage used for arrested landing trials. (FAST)

Another novel feature investigated at RAE was the 'carpet' landing system. This, it was hoped, would prevent the need for a conventional undercarriage and thereby allow seven per cent weight saving in naval fighters. Here, Royal Navy test pilot Eric Brown makes a spectacular arrival on the flexible rubber mat at Farnborough's Jersey Brow site. (BSH)

The damage incurred by Brown's Vampire did not prevent extra trials being carried out at sea on HMS *Warrior*, but the system was judged to be 'non cost effective' and was not proceeded with. (BSH)

In 1945, a number of captured German aircraft were evaluated by a special team of Service pilots based at Farnborough. This is the Dornier D335A which was potentially the fastest piston-engined fighter ever built. This particular machine crashed at Cove near Farnborough killing Gp Capt. Hards, CO of the Enemy Aircraft Evaluation Flight. (FAST)

The Junkers 290A was also put through its paces at Farnborough. It saw a great deal of Luftwaffe service in the maritime reconnaissance and transport roles, having a range in excess of 3,500 miles. (FAST)

Despite wearing RAF markings, this captured Heinkel HE219 Uhu (Owl) bears the unmistakable stamp of German design. Judged by many to be the Luftwaffe's best night fighter, it was the first German operational aircraft to feature a nose wheel undercarriage and the world's first operational aircraft to be fitted with an ejector seat. The hardware projecting from the nose is the FuG 220 Lichtenstein SN-2 radar aerial array. (FAST)

Shown here in more detail is the search radar and 20mm MG 151/20 cannon mounted in the nose of the Enemy Aircraft Flight Messerschmitt Me410 Hornisse (Hornet). (FAST)

This Arado 232B Tausendfüssler (Millipede) was used extensively by Farnborough's Service team for ferrying equipment to and from Germany in the immediate post-war period. (FAST)

A spotters dream! This line up of service and civil aircraft was photographed at Farnborough in June 1946. Note the Seafire IIC mounted on the catapult structure on the extreme right. (FAST)

The Bristol Brabazon, which was thought to point the way ahead for air travel in the late 1940s, proved to be obsolete before it first flew. It nevertheless made an impressive spectacle as it came in to land at the 1949 SBAC show. Cody's tree is in the foreground. (BSH)

Gracing the skies over Farnborough, the RAF's crack display team, the 'Black Arrows', flying Hawker Hunter F6s, made its SBAC show debut in 1957. (FAST)

Taking over from the Hunter display team, nine English Electric Lightnings from No.74 Squadron provided thunderous aerobatics over Farnborough in 1961. (FAST)

Lined up for public inspection prior to the flying display is this interesting selection at the 1960 SBAC show. De Havilland Comet 2E XN453 and Avro Lincoln B2 G-29-1 used by Napier for icing research, dominate the foreground. (FAST)

Seen in November 1975, this Avro Shackleton 'wings' its way into Farnborough with the starboard inner propellers providing a less gaudy impression than their colleagues. (FAST)

Not all of Farnborough's activities are concerned with actual flying hardware. Here, the Q12 twenty-four foot wind tunnel originally built in 1934 was used for testing complete aircraft, engines and equipment over a period of sixty-five years. (FAST)

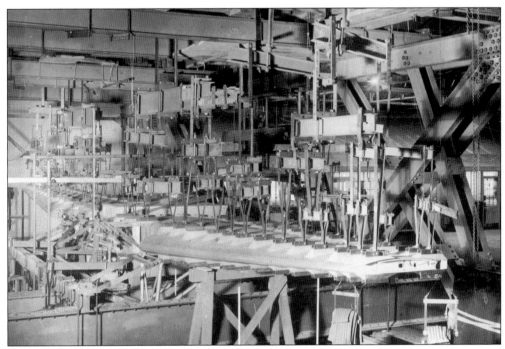

Beneath the forest of mechanical linkages, a Mosquito wing undergoes typical structural testing at Farnborough. (BSH)

Shown just after the Second World War in the hangar that now houses the BAE Systems Heritage Archive are a pair of V-1 flying bombs and the rear section of a V-2 rocket. Reconstruction of a V-2 that was recovered in Sweden, was undertaken at Farnborough in August 1944, just one month before the first of these terror weapons descended on the UK. (BSH)

# Seven

# Pioneer Profiles

Over the years a considerable number of notable personalities and their machines that have led the way in aviation have caught the public eye on momentous visits to Hampshire. Here, just a few serve to represent the many.

Following his epic flight across the Atlantic, Charles Lindbergh landed his *Spirit of St. Louis* at Gosport on 31 May 1927. (FH)

H.J. 'Bert' Hinkler served as a test pilot for Avro at Hamble and achieved international celebrity status as a long distance flyer. Thousands turned out at Eastleigh (Atlantic Park) to welcome his return after flying solo across the South Atlantic in 1931. His many record-breaking flights included, most famously, a solo flight from England to Australia in under sixteen days in 1928. (FH/PNC)

Although much to her annoyance that she was not allowed to actually pilot the aircraft, Amelia Earhart became the first woman to cross the Atlantic in 1928. The *Friendship* is shown arriving at Imperial Airways Woolston base after the flight from Newfoundland. However, Amelia Earhart did later, on 20-21 May 1932, become the first woman to make a solo crossing of the Atlantic. (FH)

In May 1930, the mighty Dornier Do-X landed at Southampton. The twelve-engined leviathan, under the command of Captain Freidrich Christiansen, was attempting a record-breaking flight from Lake Constance to New York via Rio de Janeiro. But a record of sorts was achieved when, due to malfunctions and extended repairs, the flight took ten months! (FH)

Colonel Lindbergh, this time accompanied by his wife, again visited Southampton in October 1933. On this occasion it was a stopping-point in a long distance survey flight that eventually embraced twenty-one countries and 30,000 miles. Here Lindbergh is seen greasing the propeller hub of his Lockheed Sirius float plane *Tingmissartoq* (a Greenland eskimo expression for 'The man who flies like a big bird'). (AC)

Sir Alan Cobham made regular visits to Hampshire during both his municipal Aerodrome Campaign of 1929 and his National Aviation Day Display tours of 1932-1935. (AC)

The largest machine operated in the Cobham display was the Handley Page Clive (*Astra*). Seen here in 1935 is Cobham's team of pilots, and (seated) parachutists. (AC)

Accidents did happen. On 30 June 1934, Cobham's ace stunt flier Jock McKay paid the final price when his Avro 504K crashed near Farnborough. (AC)

1935 was the year M. Henri Mignet visited Eastleigh in a bid to boost his 'Pou du Ciel' or 'Sky Louse', albeit shown here as the 'Fleeing Fly' – the light aeroplane it was said that anyone could build in his backyard. Britain, having become the first country to de-control the manufacture of light aircraft, saw many enthusiasts take up the challenge often with unfortunate results. (AC)

A sight never to be forgotten took place on 6 July 1936 when the German airship *Hindenburg* drifted majestically over the Hampshire coast en route to America. (FH/PNC)

In 1939, Maj. Alexander de Seversky demonstrated his latest pursuit plane to Air Ministry and RAF personnel at Eastleigh. Later in the year he also visited Germany with a view to selling his fighter to the Luftwaffe. In the course of his European tour, he became the first man to fly both the Spitfire and the ME109. His own machine was soon to be developed into the Republic Thunderbolt, many of which flew from Hampshire's wartime airfields. (FH/PNC)